Medjugorje Prepare the World for My Final Coming

by the Community of Caritas
with Special Contributions from
A Friend of Medjugorje

SPECIAL STATEMENT

Caritas of Birmingham is not acting on behalf of the Catholic Church or placing its mission under the church. Its mission is to reach all people of the earth. Its actions are outside of the church done privately. It is further stated:

So as not to take for granted the credibility of the Medjugorje Apparitions, it is stated that the Medjugorje apparitions are not formally approved by the Catholic Church.

Medjugorje Status
September 21, 2015 A.D.

No attempt is intended to pre-empt the Church on the validity of the Medjugorje Apparitions. They are private revelation waiting the Church's final judgment[1]. In the interim, these private revelations **are** allowed by, and for, the faithful to have devotion to and to be spread legally by the Church. Devotion and the propagation of private revelations can be forbidden only **if** the private revelation is condemned because of anything it contains which contravenes faith and morals according to AAS 58 (1966) 1186 Congregation for the Doctrine of the Faith. Medjugorje has not been condemned nor found to have anything against faith or morals, therefore it is in the grace of the Church to be followed by the faithful. By the rite of Baptism one is commissioned and given the authority to evangelize. *"By Baptism they share in the priesthood of Christ, in his prophetic and royal mission."*[2] One does not need approval to promote or to have devotions to private revelations or to spread them when in conformity to AAS 58 (1966) 1186, as the call to evangelize is given when baptized. These apparitions have not been approved formally by the Church. Caritas of Birmingham, the Community of Caritas and all associated with it, realize and accept that the final authority regarding the Queen of Peace, Medjugorje and happenings related to the apparitions, rests with the Holy See in Rome. We at Caritas, willingly submit to that judgment. While having an amiable relationship with the Diocese of Birmingham and a friendly relationship with its bishop, Caritas of Birmingham as a lay mission is not officially connected to the Diocese of Birmingham, Alabama, just as is the Knights of Columbus.[3] The Diocese of Birmingham's official position on Caritas is neutral and holds us as Catholics in good standing.

1. The Church does not have to approve the apparitions. The Church can do as She did with the apparitions of Rue du Bac in Paris and the Miraculous Medal. The Church never approved these apparitions. She gave way to the people's widespread acceptance of the Miraculous Medal and thereby the Apparitions to St. Catherine. *Sensus Fidelium* (latin, meaning "The Sense of the Faithful"), regarding Medjugorje, is that the "sense" of the people says that "Mary is here (Medjugorje)."
2. Catechism of the Catholic Church 2nd Edition
3. The Knights of Columbus also are not officially under the Church, yet they are very Catholic. The Knights of Columbus was founded as a lay organization in 1882, with the basic Catholic beliefs. Each local council appeals to the local Ordinary to be the Chaplain. The Knights of Columbus is still a lay organization, and operates with its own autonomy.

See pages 101–104 for Pricing.

For additional copies write: **Caritas of Birmingham**
100 Our Lady Queen of Peace Drive
Sterrett, AL 35147 USA
Call 205-672-2000 press ext. 315 (24 hours a day)

Published with permission from SJP Lic. COB.
© 2016, S.J.P. Lic. C.O.B.

Table of Contents

ABOUT THE AUTHOR

The author of this book is also the author of the books <u>Words From Heaven</u>®, <u>How to Change Your Husband</u>™, <u>I See Far</u>™, <u>Look What Happened While You Were Sleeping</u>™, <u>It Ain't Gonna Happen</u>™ <u>They Fired the First Shot 2012</u>™ hundreds of short books and other publications such as the *Words of the Harvesters* and the *Caritas of Birmingham Newsletter*. He has written more on Medjugorje and its messages than anyone in the world, producing life-changing writings and spiritual direction to countless numbers across the world, of all nationalities. He wishes to be known only as "A Friend of Medjugorje." The author is not one looking in from the outside regarding Medjugorje, but one who is close to the events — many times, right in the middle of the events about which he has written; a first-hand witness.

Originally writing to only a few individuals in 1987, readership has grown to over 250,000 in the United States, with additional readers in over one hundred thirty foreign countries, who follow the spiritual insights and direction given through these writings.

The author, when asked why he signs only as "A Friend of Medjugorje," stated:

> *"I have never had an ambition or desire to write.*
> *I do so only because God has shown me, through*
> *prayer, that He desires this of me. So from the*
> *beginning, when I was writing to only a few*
> *people, I prayed to God and promised I would not*
> *sign anything; that the writings would have to*

*carry themselves and not be built on a personality.
I prayed that if it was God's desire for these
writings to be inspired and known, then He could
do it by His Will and grace and that my will be
abandoned to it.*

*"The Father has made these writings known and contin-
ues to spread them to the ends of the earth. These
were Our Lord's last words before ascending: **"Be a
witness to the ends of the earth."** These writings give
testimony to that desire of Our Lord to be a witness
with one's life. It is not important to be known. It is
important to do God's Will."*

For those who require "ownership" of these writings by the
author in seeing his name printed on this work in order to
give it more credibility, we state that we cannot reconcile the
fact that these writings are producing hundreds of thousands
of conversions, if not millions through grace, and are
requested worldwide from every corner of the earth. The
author, therefore, will not take credit for a work that, by proof
of the impact these writings have to lead hearts to conversion,
have been Spirit–inspired with numbers increasing yearly,
sweeping as a wave across the ocean. Indeed in this case,
crossing every ocean of the earth. Our Lady gave this author
a direct message for him through the visionary, Marija, of
Medjugorje, in which Our Lady said to him to witness not
with words but through humility. It is for this reason that he
wishes to remain simply "A Friend of Medjugorje."

— Caritas of Birmingham

Medjugorje

The Story in Brief

A VILLAGE SEES THE LIGHT is the title of a story which "Reader's Digest" published in February 1986. It was the first major news on a mass public scale that told of the Virgin Mary visiting the tiny village of Medjugorje, Bosnia-Hercegovina. At that time this village was populated by 400 families.

It was June 24, 1981, the Feast of John the Baptist, the proclaimer of the coming Messiah. In the evening, around 5:00 p.m., the Virgin Mary appeared to two young people, Mirjana Dragičević* and Ivanka Ivanković*. Around 6:40 p.m. the same day, Mirjana and Ivanka, along with four more young people, Milka Pavlović*, the little sister of Marija, Ivan Ivanković, Vicka Ivanković*, and Ivan Dragičević saw the Virgin Mary. The next day, June 25, 1981, along with Mirjana, Ivanka, Vicka and Ivan Dragičević, Marija Pavlović* and Jakov Čolo also saw the Virgin Mary, bringing the total to six visionaries. Milka Pavlović* and Ivan Ivanković only saw Our Lady once, on that first day. These six have become known as and remain "the visionaries."

---

* Names at the time of the apparitions, they are now married with last names changed.

These visionaries are not related to one another. Three of the six visionaries no longer see Our Lady on a daily basis. As of July 2016, the Virgin is still appearing everyday to the remaining three visionaries; that's well over 15,397 apparitions.

The supernatural event has survived all efforts of the Communists to put a stop to it, many scientific studies, and even the condemnation by the local bishop; yet, the apparitions have survived, giving strong evidence that this is from God because nothing and no one has been able to stop it. For over thirty-five years, the apparitions have proved themselves over and over and now credibility is so favorable around the world that the burden of proof that this is authentic has shifted from those who believe to the burden of proof that it is not happening by those opposed to it. Those against the apparitions are being crushed by the fruits of Medjugorje — millions and millions of conversions which are so powerful that they are changing and will continue to change the whole face of the earth.

See **mej.com** for more information.
or **Medjugorje.com**

CHAPTER ONE

Prepare the World for My Final Coming

A young Carmelite nun by the name of Sr. Mary of St. Peter, in Tours, France in the 1840's, received a series of revelations from Jesus about a powerful devotion He wanted established, starting in France, and spread throughout the world. It became known as the devotion to His Holy Face, which included a prayer that Jesus dictated to Sr. Mary, *the Golden Arrow*. This devotion was eventually approved by the Church, the purpose of which was:

> *"…to make reparation for the blasphemies and outrages of 'Revolutionary men' (the Communists) — through whom God is allowing the world to be chastised for its unbelief — as well as for the blasphemies of atheists and freethinkers and others, plus, for blasphemy and the profanation of Sundays by Christians."* [1]

Jesus made this chosen nun understand that this was an urgent matter, as God could not endure the endless assault against His Name and the day He commanded to be kept Holy. Jesus gave her instructions to relay His requests to her superiors and to Her bishop. He wanted the prayers He dictated to her to be spread and prayed by the faithful. He told Sr. Mary that the prayers needed more than just having them printed and given out. Souls needed their interest "stimulated." Sr. Mary of St. Peter wrote to her superiors:

> *"Our Lord made me understand that a mere printing of the prayers alone would never suffice, but that it was necessary to add an explanation* **throwing light on the end which the Work had in view.** *The Savior told me that in order to* **stimulate** *[rouse or excite to action]* **the interest of the Faithful** *to say these prayers to the glory of the Holy Name of God,* **it was essential to instruct them concerning the designs of God in this great Work,** *for only then when this would be done through the means of adequate printed matter would we see pious souls* **feasting themselves on these prayers as bees feast upon flowers.** *He then revealed to me that* **these prayers would be very instrumental in obtaining the conversion of sinners."** [2]

We have entered the Extraordinary Year of Mercy that Pope Francis initiated on December 8, 2015. Yet the majority of Catholics know nothing, or understand little, concerning the great graces available in this Jubilee Year, namely, that by receiving a very special plenary indulgence, you receive a complete remission of all temporal punishment due to sin. Using the words of Jesus to Sr. Mary, the faithful's *"interest has not been stimulated."* It is *"necessary to add an explanation throwing light on the end which the Work* [in this case, Our Lady's apparitions in Medjugorje and the Divine Mercy revelations] *had in view."* Even we, the apostles of Our Lady, must stop and seriously reflect, not only on what opportunity is being given to us **in this moment of time** for the conversion of ourselves and our families, but what our responsibility is before God and Our Lady to be interceding "unceasingly" for mercy for our nations and our world. Before we can "instruct the ignorant," which is one of the seven spiritual works of mercy, in *"the designs of God in this great Work,"* it is essential that we, ourselves, become the *"pious souls feasting themselves on these prayers* [and revelations] *as bees feast upon flowers."* In our time, it is the messages of Our Lady, first and foremost, that we are to be "feasting" upon, living and spreading Our Lady to all we meet, as She is the ultimate gift of Mercy for mankind today.

What happens when we don't answer the call of Heaven, or answer it, but without great fervor? What happens when man fails to recognize the time of God's visitation, fails to recognize the signs of the times? History has many examples we can ponder, of which only a few will be mentioned here.

Our Lady's Apparitions in Rwanda — 1989

In 2012, Caritas published A Friend of Medjugorje's book, They Fired the First Shot 2012TM, in which he reflected upon the great danger of ignoring Heaven's warnings. An excerpt from the book follows:

> "Do you think that apparitions every day for 31 years, as of June 25, 2012, are for insignificant reasons concerning the future of the world? Can we say, 'Well, Our Lady is here. She will take care of everything?' Then why does Our Lady say:
>
> March 21, 1985
>
> **"Dear children, I wish to keep on giving messages and, therefore, today I call you to live and accept my messages...I call on you – accept me, dear children, that it might go well with you..."**
>
> Did you know that before the Rwanda massacre, Our Lady was there, appearing in the small village of Kibeho in Rwanda? Do you

think when Our Lady of Kibeho appeared in 1982 to seven visionaries, and gave a warning to pray and repent, repeatedly warning them of the blood bath coming, that She did so to save everyone physically? Did you know the Catholic Church approved these apparitions, yet three of the seven visionaries were killed in the genocide? Being a visionary did not spare them. Did you know that Our Lady, during the Kibeho apparitions, taught one of the visionaries a song, and when she got to one part of the song, Our Lady stopped her to teach and emphasize the following words? Our Lady made her repeat the following words seven times:

"There will be fire that will come from beneath the earth and consume everything on earth...The day You will come to take those who have served You, God, we beg You to have mercy on us..."

Fire did come out of the ground, the fire of hell by the sword. Do you think this song just applies to Rwanda? Will it also apply to a world now gone mad? Stop and seriously consider the following words Our Lady gave in Medjugorje recently:

August 2, 2011

"…As individuals, my children, you cannot stop the evil that wants to begin to rule in this world and to destroy it…"

…Our Lady warned both the Hutus and Tutsis in Rwanda, through Her apparitions in Kibeho, telling them not to hate. It was foreshown by Her in the Medjugorje apparitions… but Our Lady could not help them. On April 24, 1994, 19 days into what would be more than 100 days of the Rwanda genocide, Our Lady gave Her monthly message to Medjugorje visionary Marija. Our Lady said:

"…if you do not pray and if you are not humble and obedient to the messages I am giving you, <u>I cannot help you</u>…" [3]

End of Excerpt from <u>They Fired the First Shot 2012</u>™

What was written above by A Friend of Medjugorje concerning Rwanda can also be applied to the many other times Our Lady and/or Our Lord appeared to individuals over the past several centuries to repeatedly warn man to return to God. Consider a few other examples:

St. Margaret Mary & France — 1689–1789

Jesus appeared to Sr. Margaret Mary in the year **1689** requesting the King of France to consecrate France to the Sacred Heart of Jesus. He warned that great harm would come if the consecration did not take place. Nonetheless, Heaven's request was ignored. Exactly 100 years later, in **1789**, the citizens of France, in an act of mutiny, took upon themselves legislative powers, apart from the King, which gave birth to the French Revolution. As has happened so many times before in Church history, her shepherds were "a day late and a dollar short." Even Louis XVI and his wife, Marie Antoinette, were publicly dethroned, imprisoned and guillotined, as were thousands of bishops, priests, religious and laity. King Louis, after he was imprisoned, promised to consecrate France to the Sacred Heart if he regained his freedom, but it was too late to avert the tidal wave of terror and bloodshed that swept through France, in which the Church, itself, became targeted for destruction.

Sr. Mary of St. Peter & France — 1843 to 1848

Sr. Mary was warned that if enough prayers were not said for reparation against the sins of blasphemy and the breaking of the Sabbath, France, again, would experience divine punishment. Shortly after this warning was given, a great flood almost destroyed the city of Tours. That was only the beginning. Sr. Mary said, after the flood:

> *"Our Lord communicated to me that this time He would use as the instruments of punishment, not the elements, but **'the malice of revolutionary men.'"** On February 13, 1848, Jesus again spoke to Sr. Mary saying that **"terrible woes were impending...Pray, pray, for the Church is threatened by a fearful tempest!'** The Savior made me understand that His justice was greatly irritated against mankind for its sins but particularly for those that directly outrage the Majesty of God — that is, Communism, Atheism, cursing, and the desecration of Sundays."[4]*

On February 20, 1848, *"a serious revolution in Paris shook the very foundations of the French government and all of Europe. King Louis Philippe, who after eighteen years felt himself securely established as monarch of France, was forced to flee with his family into exile."* [5]

St. Faustina & Poland — 1924–1938

Jesus chose St. Faustina to be His apostle of Divine Mercy, as well as a victim soul to offer reparation for the sins of Poland and of the world. Pope John Paul II said:

> *"Right from the beginning of my ministry in St. Peter's See in Rome, I considered this message [of Divine Mercy] my special task. Providence has assigned it to me in the present situation of man, the Church and the world. It could be said that precisely this situation assigned that message to me as my task before God."* [6]

Jesus taught Sr. Faustina the depth of His great mercy for all His creatures, yet there were consequences if man did not pay heed to His entreaties. Of Poland, Sr. Faustina wrote:

> *"I saw the anger of God hanging heavy over Poland. And now I see that if God were to visit our country with the greatest chastisements that would still be great mercy because, for such grave transgressions, He could punish us with eternal annihilation. I was paralyzed with fear when the Lord lifted the veil a little for me..."* [1533] [7]

St. Faustina actually revealed part of the 3rd Secret of Fatima, concerning the angel sending fire to the earth, which is deflected by the splendor of Our Lady. St. Faustina explains:

"In the evening, I saw the Mother of God, with Her breast bared and pierced with a sword. She was shedding bitter tears and shielding us against God's terrible punishment. <u>God wants to inflict terrible punishment on us, but He cannot because the Mother of God is shielding us.</u> Horrible fear seized my soul. I kept praying incessantly for Poland, for my dear Poland, which is so lacking in gratitude for the Mother of God. If it were not for the Mother of God, all our efforts would be of little use…" [686] [8]

Again, Jesus speaks of raining fire down, like what Sodom and Gomorrah received:

"One day Jesus told me that He would cause a chastisement to fall upon the most beautiful city in our country [probably Warsaw]. This chastisement would be that with which God had punished Sodom and Gomorrah.* …After a moment, Jesus said to me, **'My child, unite yourself closely to Me during the Sacrifice and offer My Blood and My Wounds to My Father in expiation for the sins of that city…"** [9]

---

* As Sodom and Gomorrah were destroyed by the falling of "brimstone and fire from the Lord out of Heaven" (see Gen 19:24), so Warsaw was indeed destroyed during World War II, as were many Polish towns, by incendiary and demolition bombs dropped from aircraft.

Lucia, Jacinta & Francesco — Fatima, Russia & the World — 1917

In Portugal, in 1917, the Virgin Mary appeared to three shepherd children, Lucia, Jacinta & Francesco, while World War I continued to rage on. On July 13, 1917, Our Lady said to the three children:

> **"...If what I say to you is done, many souls will be saved and there will be peace. The war is going to end, but if people do not cease offending God, a worse one will break out...When you see a night illuminated by an unknown light, know that this is the great sign given you by God that He is about to punish the world for its crimes by means of wars, famine, and persecution of the Church and of the Holy Father."**

Our Lady continued on how to avoid the perils facing the earth:

> **"To prevent this I shall come to ask for the consecration of Russia to My Immaculate Heart, and the Communion of Reparation on the First Saturdays. If My requests are heeded, Russia will be converted and there will be peace; if not,**

she will spread her errors throughout the world, causing wars and persecutions of the Church. The good will be martyred, the Holy Father will have much to suffer, various nations will be annihilated..."

True to Her word, Our Lady appeared to Lucia, then a cloistered nun, on June 13, 1929, in which She came to ask for the consecration of Russia:

"The moment has come in which God asks the Holy Father, in union with all the bishops of the world, to make the consecration of Russia to My Immaculate Heart, promising to save it by this means. There are so many souls whom the Justice of God condemns for sins committed against Me, that I have come to ask reparation: sacrifice yourself for this intention and pray." [10]

Expressing Our Lady's wish to her spiritual father, Sr. Lucia also revealed what Our Lady had promised if the consecration was fulfilled by the Holy Father:

*"The Good Lord promises to end the persecution in Russia (the Bolshevik revolution) **if** the Holy Father will himself make a solemn act of reparation and consecration of Russia to the Sacred*

*Hearts of Jesus and Mary, as well as **ordering all the bishops of the Catholic world to do the same,** and if the Holy Father promises that upon the ending of this persecution he will approve and recommend the practice of the reparatory devotion already described."* [11]

We know, of course, that the Consecration was not done when Our Lady requested it. One hundred million deaths and the annihilation of nations all could have been avoided. We know this as a result of the lack of obedience to Our Lady's words. In the same year that the above message was given by Our Lady to Sr. Lucy, in 1929, Josef Stalin began to starve to death the people of the Ukraine. This alone led to 10,000,000 to 15,000,000 deaths. Stalin enacted a new Communist law, the separation of Church and State, which was used to justify not only high taxes but the arrest, imprisonment, exile and even execution of priests and bishops. This purification did not have to happen. Can it happen again? Our Lady of Medjugorje is ignored by most of the Church structure. In 1917, there were 6,000,000 Catholics in Russia; by 1939 there were less than half a million. According to The Red Book of the Persecuted Church, *"The years 1929-1932 saw the total liquidation of the Catholic hierarchy in the Soviet Union."* Between July 1 and September 1, 1936, approximately eight thousand religious were murdered: 12 bishops, over 5,000 priests, more than 2,000 monks, and hundreds of nuns and novices. Our Lady of Medjugorje, as in the past, is yet again trying to avoid the future purification of those in the Church. Yet, the very ones who will be the first to suffer, will be the last to realize they could have avoided their demise by fully endorsing what Our Lady is directing through Medjugorje.

There was still worse to come with the advent of World War II. When the Nazi's invaded the Ukraine and Russia in the early 1940's, they began a systematic elimination of the entire Jewish population, in which more than 1.5 million Jews were killed. This was the precursor of what was to happen throughout all of Europe, in which more than six million Jews were martyred. The world had never seen such hatred and disregard of human life. Mankind crossed a line and the spread of evil ideologies, of which **Our Lady had warned, as Our Lady in Medjugorje warns today**, unleashed unrest, fear, hatred, division, destruction, war, unbelief, death, the rejection of moral absolutes, which led to the destruction of the highest form of social living, the family. Above all, it led to hatred towards and rejection of God. The famous Soviet dissident, Aleksandr Solzhenitsyn, who had spent eight years in a Soviet gulag (prison), and who eventually escaped to the United

States, for years studied to find the root cause that led to the immense atrocities committed against humanity in his beloved Motherland, Russia. All his study and research led him to one defining conclusion. He wrote:

"Over a half century ago, while I was still a child, I recall hearing a number of old people offer the following explanation for the great disasters that had befallen Russia: **'Men have forgotten God; that's why all this has happened.'** *Since then I have spent well-nigh 50 years working on the history of our revolution; in the process I have read hundreds of books, collected hundreds of personal testimonies, and have already contributed eight volumes of my own toward the effort of clearing away the rubble left by that upheaval. But if I were asked today to formulate as concisely as possible the main cause of the ruinous revolution that swallowed up some 60 million of our people, I could not put it more accurately than to repeat:* **'Men have forgotten God; that's why all this has happened.'"** [12]

In Medjugorje, Our Lady said of our day:

October 25, 2006

"...You are not conscious, little children, that God is giving you a great opportunity

to convert and to live in peace and love. You are so blind and attached to earthly things and think of earthly life. God sent me to lead you toward eternal life. I, little children, am not tired, although I see that your hearts are heavy and tired for everything that is a grace and a gift...

But This is the Time of Mercy, Why Speak of Judgement Now?

How well we live the time of Mercy will directly impact what will happen in the time of God's Justice. St. Faustina was told by Jesus:

"In the Old Covenant I sent prophets wielding thunderbolts to My people. Today I am sending you with My mercy to the people of the whole world. I do not want to punish aching mankind, but I desire to heal it, pressing it to My Merci-

ful Heart. I use punishment when they themselves force Me to do so; My hand is reluctant to take hold of the sword of justice. Before the Day of Justice I am sending the Day of Mercy." [13]

Archbishop Fulton J. Sheen once said:

"A man may stand for the justice of God, but a woman stands for His Mercy." [14]

This is who Our Lady is; She is the Mercy of God, the Mother of Mercy—our life, our sweetness and our hope. She, who has been sent everyday for almost 35 years, has revealed the love and mercy of God as no other has, yet She also warns of a time of justice coming. But God's justice is also mercy because it prevents men from going to hell when they call out to God for His mercy in the midst of great crisis and turmoil. However, the point of this writing is not to focus on God's coming justice, but to motivate and inspire believers in this time of Mercy to bend God to our hearts in begging for mercy now and for the future. As we have studied nations under judgement in past history, such as France and Poland, consider one other nation, namely Portugal. It was in this country that Our Lady appeared in Fatima, and Our Lady spoke to her young visionaries about Portugal's future.

Concerning Fatima's three visionaries of Portugal, Jacinta, one of the three, before her death, informed her bishop that the Blessed Virgin prophesied **"a civil war of an anarchist or communist character"** that would erupt in Portugal unless **"there were souls who would do penance and make reparation for the offenses done to God..."** [15]

Notice in the following — What results when Bishops Respond Immediately to Our Lady

On May 13, 1931, all of Portugal's bishops consecrated Portugal to the Immaculate Heart of Mary. This was at a time when freemasonry and bolshevism were battling to gain supremacy over Catholicism's influence on the nation.

Following the Consecration, a Catholic man born of peasant stock, Antonio Salazar, won the 1933 election to become the head of the Portuguese government. It was considered a miracle that he won. Not only Salazar, but many believed that it was through the intercession of the Virgin Mary, **through the consecration of Portugal's bishops, in obedience to Heaven's command** that led to this victory in defeating freemasonry and bolshevism. In 1935, Salazar banned freemasonry from Portugal, which almost cost him his life. *Would Our Lady not have done the same for Russia, had the Consecration been done as She asked?* In the summer of 1931, Our Lord told Lucy concerning Russia's consecration:

> **"<u>They</u> did not want to heed My request. Like the King of France, they will repent and do so, <u>but it will be late</u>. Russia will have already spread her errors throughout the world, causing wars and persecutions of the Church. The Holy Father will have much to suffer."** [16]

The Queen of Peace of Medjugorje is here, yet many in the Church continue to see it as inconsequential. Do we now understand what opportunity is before us in this Year of Mercy? Yet another chance. Consider this specific time we are living in:

The Extraordinary Year of Mercy is the culmination of events that began with the revelations of Divine Mercy to St. Faustina in the 1930's. In the whole history of the Church, there have only been three other times in which an "Extraordinary Jubilee" was named—which makes one understand that Pope Francis, himself, understands the significance of this time. Pope Francis, when addressing the priests of the Diocese of Rome on March 6, 2014, stated:

"Listen to the voice of the Spirit that speaks to the whole Church in this our time, which is, in fact, the time of mercy. I am certain of this…We have been living in the time of mercy for 30 or more years, up to now. It is the time of mercy in the whole Church. It was instituted by St. John Paul II. He had the 'intuition' that this was the time of mercy. We think of the beatification and canonization of Sister Faustina Kowalska; then he introduced the Feast of Divine Mercy. He moved slowly, slowly, and went ahead with this."

Pope Francis continues:

"In the homily for the Canonization, which took place in 2000, John Paul II stressed that Jesus Christ's message to Sister Faustina was placed in time between two World Wars and is very linked to the history of the 20th century. How will the future of man be on earth, [John Paul] says."

Pope Francis **then quoted Pope John Paul II** concerning what man's future will be on earth:

"'It is not given to us to know it. It is true, however, that along with the new progresses we will not lack painful experiences. However, the light of Divine Mercy, which the Lord wished virtually to give again to the world through the charism of Sister Faustina, will illumine the path of the men of the third millennium.'

Pope Francis continues:

"It is clear. It was explicit in 2000, but it was something that had been maturing in [John Paul's] heart for some time. He had this intuition in his prayer...Today we forget everything too hastily, also the Magisterium of the Church! It is inevitable in part, but we cannot forget the great contents, the great intuitions and the consignment left to the People of God. And that of the Divine Mercy is one of these. It is a consignment that [John Paul] gave us, but which comes from on High. It is up to us, as ministers of the Church, to keep alive this message..."

Jesus attached great graces, like never before, to the three o'clock Hour of Mercy,* Prayer of Divine Mercy, Divine Mercy Chaplet, the Feast of Divine Mercy (first Sunday after Easter), the Divine Mercy Image & the Novena of Divine Mercy all of which Pope John Paul II gave the Church's blessing upon. The Extraordinary Year of Mercy, as announced by Pope Francis, adds turbo-fire to all the above.

- Following the Year of Mercy is the 100th anniversary of the apparitions of Our Lady of Fatima, May 13, 2017—possibly ending the 100 years that satan had requested of God to try the Church, as revealed by Our Lady in Medjugorje to visionary Mirjana. Our Lady said that when the secrets begin to take place, of which three are admonishments to the world because the world did not repent, satan's power will be destroyed. But the upheaval caused by the systems of man falling, which satan has spent more than a

---

* Medjugorje visionary Marija came to Caritas in September, 2014 to celebrate the Feast of the Exaltation of the Cross, September 14, 2014, one year after the Cross was constructed and then consecrated on June 30, 2013. On the vigil of the feast day of the Exaltation of the Cross, September 13, 2014, Marija asked Our Lady in the apparition, *"If it is possible to have some special apparition over at Cross Mountain?"* and to bless the Cross. To the great surprise and awe of everyone present, Marija said, *"Our Lady smiled and said, 'Yes, She will come tomorrow at 3 o'clock.'"* It was Our Lady's request that we meet at the Cross at 3:00 P.M. for Her apparition—the Hour of Divine Mercy. Though Our Lady has had 189 apparitions here on the grounds of Caritas, and has appeared at many various times throughout the days, never had there been an apparition at 3:00 P.M. This has great significance of the time and recognition of Christ's death at 3:00 P.M.

century building up, will cause much chaos and crisis in the world.

- On record for over 25 years, A Friend of Medjugorje has believed that Our Lady's "daily" apparitions in Medjugorje will last for 40 years—the time it took for Moses to lead his people through the desert. Our Lady is leading us, also, into a new time. The year 2021 is the 40th year of the apparitions—just five years from now. We believe these are critical years for the fulfillment of Our Lady's plans through Medjugorje.

- The "Signs of the Time" compel us to believe that God is on the move, and that we must ready ourselves for great events to take place in the world.

This Year a Critical Opportunity Is Within Your Grasp

What Is This Year of Mercy About?

It is yet another effort of Heaven to *"stimulate our interest"* in the work of reparation for the sins of the world—for our own future. Our Lady told Mirjana that when you pray for nonbelievers, you are praying for your own future. Mirjana said to a group of English pilgrims in Medjugorje on October 17, 2007:

> *Our Lady is asking from us to put in our daily prayers in the first place the prayer for unbelievers because Our Lady has been emphasizing that most of the bad things in the world like wars, crime, abortion, are coming from unbelievers. Because of that, Our Lady says that when you pray for them, you in fact are praying for yourselves and your own futures.*

Through our prayers, our sacrifices, our begging Our Lady's intercession for mercy, we are giving God what is necessary to lessen the penalties of sin for our own nations. Jesus said to St. Faustina, as she was praying for Poland one day:

> **'I bear a special love for Poland, and <u>if she will be obedient to My will</u>, I will exalt her in might and holiness. From her will come forth the spark that will prepare the world for My final coming.'' [17]**

Poland was devastated during the war, but God resurrected Poland and used her, through her son, Pope John Paul II, to give freedom to the movements of God that is allowing His mercy to be recognized and embraced today. Yes, this is through the Divine Mercy revelations, but also,

Pope John Paul II saved Medjugorje on more than one occasion, and throughout his entire pontificate always encouraged the faithful to go there, while counseling the bishops and priests to give freedom to Medjugorje as it was producing conversions by the millions. And there can be no question, as A Friend of Medjugorje has voiced since the 1980's, that Our Lady of Medjugorje has come to **"prepare the world for Her Son's final coming."** While some may have started to believe it, A Friend of Medjugorje has paved the way for many to begin to open their hearts to see it as preparation for Her Son's return. When A Friend of Medjugorje was asked when will it be, he responded:

> *"It may be 5 years, 50 years or 500 years from now. We do not know. But one thing we do know is that Our Lady is here in Medjugorje preceding and preparing the world for the Second Coming of Her Son."*

In the interim, there is a lot of work to be done and a redoubling of our efforts for prayer and reparation in repentance for our own sins and the sins of the world.

In the case of Sister Mary of St. Peter, when Christ warned of the trouble coming to France, she redoubled her zeal in making reparation, to the point she was praying almost unceasingly. She wrote:

"The Lord has told me that in consequence of the initial efforts made to establish somewhat the Work of Reparation, our country which was to be almost entirely destroyed by the darts of His justice, would now only be partly punished by the terrible flames of His anger. Oh, how I long to entreat all the Bishops to establish the Work of the Reparation in their dioceses." [18]

And Our Lady told the Fatima visionaries that when the Consecration of Russia takes place and through the prayers of expiation that Her followers continually recite that:

"In the end, My Immaculate Heart will triumph. The Holy Father will consecrate Russia to me, and a certain period of peace will be granted to the world." [19]

Believers often use Our Lady's above words as an excuse to remain complacent and inactive in working for the salvation of souls, knowing that "in the end" Our Lady will be given the victory. A Friend of Medjugorje becomes indignant when he hears this. He responds, *"But how many souls will be lost eternally in the meantime because of not having enough generous souls willing to sacrifice, witness to and pray for their conversion?"* St. Faustina once asked Jesus how He could tolerate so

many sins and crimes and not punish them? The Lord
answered her:

> **"I have eternity for punishing** [these]**, and
> so I am prolonging the time of mercy for
> the sake of** [sinners]**. But woe to them
> if they do not recognize this time of My
> visitation."** [20]

We know the Year of Mercy has grace attached
to it that is unbounded. It is tied to the understanding of Jubilee—designated years in which all spiritual
debts are remitted, where forgiveness and reconciliation is sought after and granted, and where prisoners
are set free. Yet few really understand the spiritual
ramifications of Jubilee years. It is up to those who
understand—to spread this knowledge in every way
imaginable. We must also be willing to take upon ourselves the expiation of the sins of nonbelievers, to help
win for them the grace of reconciliation with God. The
Church gives the formulas, the "rules" for how to obtain
an indulgence—but this isn't sufficient to set souls on
fire in begging God for His mercy, which needs to happen as never before. It is we who trust in the Mercy of
God and who intercede for His Mercy that holds back
the hand of His judgment. On more than one occasion,
Jesus said to St. Faustina:

"For your sake I withhold the hand which punishes; for your sake I bless the earth."

[431] [21]

Endnotes:

1. Golden Arrow: The Devotion to the Holy Face of Jesus & Revelations of Sr. Mary of St. Peter, 2010, Tan Books & Publishers
2. Ibid.
3. They Fired the First Shot 2012, A Friend of Medjugorje, 2012, Caritas of Birmingham, AL
4. Golden Arrow, 2010, Tan Books & Publishers
5. Ibid.
6. Pope John Paul II at the Shrine of Merciful Love in Covalenza, Italy, on November 22, 1981.
7. Diary of Saint Maria Faustina, Divine Mercy in My Soul, 1987, Marian Press
8. Ibid.
9. Ibid.
10. Documents on Fatima & the Memoirs of Sister Lucia; Fr. Antonio Maria Martins, S.J., 2002, Family Fatima Apostolate
11. Ibid.
12. en.wikipedia.org/wiki/Aleksandr_**Solzhenitsyn**
13. Diary of Saint Maria Faustina, Divine Mercy in My Soul, 1987, Marian Press
14. https://www.goodreads.com/author/quotes/2412.Fulton_J_Sheen
15. The Whole Truth About Fatima, Volume II, Frere Michel de la Sainte Trinite, 1989, Immaculate Heart Publications
16. Ibid.
17. Diary of Saint Maria Faustina, Divine Mercy in My Soul, 1987, Marian Press
18. Golden Arrow, 2010, Tan Books & Publishers
19. Documents on Fatima & the Memoirs of Sister Lucia, Fr. Antonio Maria Martins, S.J., 2002, Family Fatima Apostolate
20. Diary of Saint Maria Faustina, Divine Mercy in My Soul, 1987, Marian Press
21. Ibid.

CHAPTER TWO

What If It Was?

What if this was our last Christmas with Our Lady appearing in the world through Medjugorje? What if we knew that on a given day this coming year Our Lady would say this is Her last apparition? Would we think or act differently knowing that Our Lady's time was coming to a close? How would we live this Year of Mercy in which the Church has entered if we believed it was leading us towards the end of Our Lady's apparitions?

Our Lady told the Medjugorje visionaries that these apparitions are the last on earth in which one (the six visionaries) will be able to see Her, hear Her, talk to Her and touch Her. After Our Lady's apparitions in Medjugorje cease, She will never appear in this manner again on the earth. Do you think Our Lady will reveal the time of Her last visit ahead of the actual date? The three visionaries who no longer see Our Lady everyday were given only one day's notice that their daily apparitions were ending. The very next day Our Lady told them this was their last daily apparition. However, in God's mercy, Our Lady has been allowed to appear to each of these visionaries on a special day each year for the rest of their earthly lives. To Ivanka, Our Lady comes on June 25th each year, the anniversary of the beginning of Our Lady's apparitions in Medjugorje; to Jakov, Our Lady appears on Christmas Day every year and he is given the added grace of seeing Our Lady appear with Baby Jesus; and to Mirjana, Our Lady appears every year on her birthday, though Mirjana says that this day is significant not because it is her birthday, but because something remarkable will take place on this date in the future, of which we will one day see. So, if Our Lady did not forewarn her own visionaries, is it likely that She will reveal to the world the future date that will be the ending of Her apparitions? The three visionaries who no longer see Our Lady on a daily basis were devastated, even years after Our Lady stopped appearing to them. Ivan has repeatedly said that he would challenge anyone, after having just one apparition of Our Lady, to find anything interesting on the earth again.

Perhaps we will not be given any advance warning of Our Lady's final days, but there are events happening and signs being given by Heaven that should shake us from complacency and help us to "be ready" whenever that fateful day arrives. Have we, for instance, considered this Year of Mercy that the Church has just now entered? Do we understand its significance? Consider the history that led us finally to the Year of Mercy. The Divine Mercy devotion came through private revelations to a young polish nun, Sr. Faustina in the 1930's. Belief in Sr. Faustina and the Divine Mercy revelations was widely held throughout Poland. However, in 1959 a ban was placed on Faustina's diary that stopped its propagation. A polish archbishop, Karol Wojtyła, who eventually became Cardinal Wojtyła took up the cause of Faustina's saintliness which eventually led to the Vatican lifting the ban on spreading the message of Divine Mercy. That was in April, 1978. Less than six months later, in October, 1978, Cardinal Wojtyła was elected to the Chair of St. Peter and named Pope John Paul II. In November, 1981, John Paul expressed what he believed was a special task given to him to fulfill as Pope:

"Right from the beginning of my ministry in St. Peter's See in Rome, I considered this message [of Divine Mercy] my special task. Providence has assigned it to me in the present situation of man, the Church and the world. It could be said that

precisely this situation assigned that message to me as my task before God."

Jesus had told Sr. Faustina that He wanted the Church to establish the feast of Divine Mercy on the second Sunday of Easter. John Paul was the Pope who officially established this feast day in the Church. On April 30, 2000, Divine Mercy Sunday, which was also named the Year of Mercy, as it was John Paul's desire to "pass on this message [of Divine Mercy] to the third millennium," John Paul not only declared that from this time on, the second Sunday of Easter would become known as Divine Mercy Sunday, but he also canonized St. Faustina on this day. She was the first saint of the new millennium. Of this day, Pope John Paul stated, *"Today is the happiest day of my life."* On April 2, 2005, the vigil of Divine Mercy Sunday, just after hearing the Mass of Divine Mercy, John Paul II breathed his last breath in a stunningly beautiful confirmation of his life's calling and mission to establish the Divine Mercy devotion throughout the Church and the world. Mission accomplished.

What does Divine Mercy have to do with Our Lady's apparitions in Medjugorje? Our Lady's daily apparitions for over 34 years **'is' the greatest expression of**

God's Divine Mercy upon mankind today. The Heavenly Father has sent Our Lady to express, on His behalf, His merciful love to the world, to convince the world of His love, to teach the world how to live the Word of His Son.

September 2, 2015

> **"...I am a grace from the Heavenly Father, sent to help you to live the word of my Son..."**

What is the **"word of my Son"** that Our Lady wants to help us to live? Love, trust, surrender, peace, and so much more—all of which is encompassed in the Divine Mercy message. Pope John Paul II defined what mercy is in his encyclical *Dives in Misericordia*. He said "mercy" is "love's second name." Jesus is love incarnate. If Jesus is love's "first" name, then Mary is love's "second" name. If Mary brought Jesus into the world the first time, would God not send Her again to usher in the time of His Second Coming? Would it not be God's grace and mercy to grant a time of grace to the world, through Our Lady's coming, before His time of judgement? Read the words of Jesus given to St. Faustina:

> **"Speak to the world about My mercy...**
> **It is a sign for the end times. After it will**

**come the Day of Justice. While there is
still time, let them have recourse to the
fount of My mercy."**

Why is Jesus' mercy so vast, so unlimited in this time of
mercy? Because His justice will be so vast, so unlimited,
to the measure He gave out in His mercy. No one at the
moment of judgement will be able to claim Christ did
not give every chance possible to accept His leniency of
mercy to love Him. Their rejection of the Son of Mary
will be the judgment they pronounce upon themselves.
It will be horrible, beyond our capacity to measure.
We are commissioned by Jesus, via St. Faustina, and
now via Our Lady of Medjugorje, to give warning to the
world. St. Faustina tells us Jesus' words:

> **"Tell souls about this great mercy of
> Mine, because the awful day, the day of
> My justice, is near."**

Our Lady has purchased, through Her Medjugorje
visitations, more time for us. We have passed a time of
judgment. Jesus said to St. Faustina:

> **"I am prolonging the time of mercy for
> the sake of sinners. But woe to them if
> they do not recognize this time of My
> visitation."**

This Year of Mercy allows you plenary indulgences that will wipe away all of your sins and atonements by simply going through the Holy Doors of any diocesan Cathedral, the Holy Doors in St. Peter's in Rome, or any of the other cathedrals/churches designated by the Vatican.*

> **"He who refuses to pass through the door of My mercy must pass through the door of My Justice."**

Do you think because Our Lady is love, that She is not strong and would never address us with such seriousness, nor use the words "I" am "warning you"? Do not delude yourself because Her own words warn us that the time of grace God is giving to us is limited and will not continue.

Our Lady said on November 2, 2006:

> **"Dear children! My coming to you, my children, is God's love. God is sending**

---

* To obtain the Jubilee Indulgence one must make a brief pilgrimage, as a sign of the deep desire for true conversion, to the Holy Doors that will be open in every Cathedral or in Churches designated by the Diocesan Bishop, as well as in the four Papal Basilicas in Rome. The indulgence may also be obtained in the Shrines in which the Door of Mercy is open and in Churches that are traditionally identified as Jubilee Churches. To obtain the Jubilee Indulgence one must also receive the Sacrament of Confession, have celebrated the Holy Eucharist and made a reflection on mercy. One must also make the profession of faith, with prayer for the Holy Father and for the intentions of his heart for the good of the Church and of the entire world.

me to warn you and to show you the right way. Do not shut your eyes before the truth, my children. Your time is a short time. Do not permit delusions to begin to rule over you. The way on which I desire to lead you is the way of peace and love. This is the way which leads to my Son, your God..."

In that moment of transition from mercy to judgement, great will be what the book of Lamentation in Holy Scripture foretells — a time of great lamentation when judgement begins and mercy ends.

August 25, 1997

"... God gives me this time as a gift to you, so that I may instruct and lead you on the path of salvation. Dear children, now you do not comprehend this grace, but soon a time will come when you will lament for these messages. That is why, little children, live all of the words which I have given you through this time of grace..."

In the delusion of today's world, man is redefining Natural Law, placing man's law above God's, and thereby setting in motion—judgement. Indeed, it is only through

God's grace that judgement has not already happened. Look at the world. How long can God tolerate the sins that fill the earth…yet His mercy, thus far, is overriding His judgement through the love of His Mother.

December 25, 1995

> **"…I am with you and I present you to Jesus in a special way, now in this new time in which one should decide for Him. This time is the time of grace…"**

April 25, 2007

> **"… This is a time of grace while I am with you, make good use of it…"**

Change, break away from <u>everything</u> that is not of God or keeps you away from God!

October 25, 2006

> **"… Today the Lord permitted me to tell you again that you live in a time of grace. You are not conscious, little children, that God is giving you a great opportunity to convert…You are so blind and attached to earthly things and think of earthly life.**

God sent me to lead you toward eternal life..."

We are in quicksand and the hour glass is pouring out its sand. We have entered a time in which Our Lady is trying to pull us out of danger to save us, through Pope Francis, who has opened the Year of Mercy so liberally, so leniently, that many do not recognize what is happening and are upset with him. Yet, Francis holds the keys to the Church to declare a seemingly insane step of intervention, without logic, offering such forgiveness and acceptance into the Church that it is causing many to question the Holy Father. You would not question him if you contemplated how horrible will be the judgement. Jesus, through the Church and His pontiff is eliminating every claim of excuse that the judgement is not just when it comes.

August 25, 2005

> **"... God gave you a gift of this time as a time of grace. Therefore, little children, make good use of every moment..."**

Use what is granted to <u>all </u>through the Church <u>now</u>! Reconcile and convert!

February 25, 1996

"...This time is a time of grace. <u>Especially now, when the Church also is inviting you to prayer and conversion</u>..."

Though Pope John Paul II was especially chosen by Heaven to usher in the time of Divine Mercy not only in the Church but also into the world, the plans of God go beyond a single man. The span of Our Lady's apparitions in Medjugorje has so far covered three pontificates: that of Pope John Paul II, Pope Benedict XVI, and now Pope Francis. Perhaps we will see other Popes rise to the throne of St. Peter before the apparitions end. But we do know this *Extraordinary Year of Mercy* is significant in God's design, the culmination of Mercy, while the signs of the time most assuredly point to the time of judgement rapidly approaching. In Mirjana's May 2, 2009 message, Mirjana relayed that Our Lady was very sad when She spoke the following words:

"... Already for a long time I am giving you my Motherly heart and offering my Son to you. You are rejecting me. You are permitting sin to overcome you more and more. You are permitting it to master you and to take away your power of discern-

**ment. My poor children, look around you
and <u>look at the signs of the times</u>. Do you
think that you can do without God's blessing?..."**

Our Lady spoke those words six years ago. How much
deeper has the world sunk into the whirlpool of sin
since then? Our Lady said to St. Faustina:

> *"You have to speak to the world about His great
> mercy and prepare the world for the Second
> Coming of Him who will come, not as a merciful
> Savior, but as a just Judge. Oh how terrible is that
> day! <u>Determined is the day of justice, the day of
> divine wrath</u>. The angels tremble before it. Speak
> to souls about this great mercy while it is still the
> time for granting mercy."*

"Determined is the day of justice." God knows the ap-
pointed hour that will end the time of grace and bring
the hour of judgement. The fact that the visionaries are
given no prior notice to the end of their own "time of
grace" being with Our Lady, is also a "sign of the times."
We must live our lives **"ready."** The end of the Year of
Mercy leads into the 100th year anniversary of Our Lady's apparitions of Fatima. Our Lady has said that the
apparitions of Medjugorje are the fulfillment of what

She began through Her apparitions of Fatima. What Our Lady had wanted to realize "through the secrets" of Fatima, She was not able to accomplish. Therefore, **"now"** is the time, through Medjugorje, when Her plans are beginning to be "realized."

August 25, 1991

> **"...today also I invite you to prayer, now as never before when my plan has begun to be realized...I invite you to renunciation for nine days so that with your help everything I wanted to realize through the secrets I began in Fatima may be fulfilled..."**

In Fatima, Our Lady had said to her visionary, Sr. Lucia, **"Unless man repents of his sin, a larger and greater war will break out."** It didn't have to happen and would not have happened if Our Lady's words were heeded. But they were not. As She said above, "everything I wanted to realize through the secrets," yet it didn't happen, therefore Medjugorje was chosen for the place where She would fulfill Her plans.

March 21, 1985

> **"… today I call you to live and accept my messages! Dear children, I love you and in a special way I have chosen this parish, <u>one more dear to me than the others</u>, in which I have gladly remained when the Almighty sent me. Therefore, I call on you — accept me, dear children, <u>that it might go well with you</u>…"**

A Day of Judgement, though terrible, will lead to the final destruction of satan's influence that he has wielded over this past century. Our Lady said that when the secrets that She revealed to Her Medjugorje visionaries come to pass, it will destroy satan's power.

December 25, 1982

> **"…This <u>century</u> is under the power of the devil, but when the secrets confided to you come to pass, his power will be destroyed…"**

Could the century Our Lady is speaking of be the hundred years that began with Her apparitions in Fatima in 1917, which would come to an end in the year 2017? We do not believe Our Lady's apparitions in Medjugorje will end in the year 2017, but we do believe the secrets are likely to "come to pass" "soon" and that this Year of Mercy is God's last heart throb of mercy for the world in which Pope Francis has literally thrown open the doors of mercy allowing the Church, as said before, to even "err on the side of mercy."

We present again the questions that were asked at the beginning of this chapter: What if this was our last Christmas with Our Lady appearing in the world through Medjugorje? What if we knew that on a given day this coming year Our Lady would say this is Her last apparition? Would we think or act differently knowing that Our Lady's time was coming to a close? How would we live this Year of Mercy in which the Church has entered if we believed it was leading us towards the end of Our Lady's apparitions?

CHAPTER THREE

Conditions that must be present to obtain the Plenary Indulgence for The Year of Mercy

Pope Francis has called for an Extraordinary Jubilee Year of Mercy, which is only the 4th Extraordinary Jubilee Year in the history of the Church. Francis has said that his wish is *that the Jubilee be a living experience of the closeness of the Father, whose tenderness is almost tangible, so that the faith of every believer may be strengthened and thus testimony to it be ever more effective.* During the Jubilee Year of Mercy, the faithful can receive a plenary indulgence that will wipe away all of your sins and the atonement for your sins. The plenary indulgence can be obtained once each day for yourself or for a soul in purgatory, if along with the indulgenced act for the Jubilee Year, you follow the prescribed conditions:

1. Be in the state of grace at the time of the indulgenced act.

2. Confession. Confession must be within about 20 days before or after the indulgenced act.

3. Receive the Holy Eucharist. One sacramental Confession suffices for several plenary indulgences, but a separate Holy Communion and a separate prayer for the Holy Father's intentions are required for each plenary indulgence. It is appropriate, but not necessary, that the sacramental Confession and especially Holy Communion and the prayer for the Pope's intentions take place on the same day that the indulgenced work is performed; but it is sufficient that these sacred rites and prayers be carried out within several days, about 20, before or after the indulgenced act.

4. Make a Profession of Faith (The Apostle's Creed)

5. Pray for the intentions of the Holy Father, an Our Father and Hail Mary.

In the following ways, the faithful may obtain the Jubilee Indulgence during the Year of Mercy:*

1. Make a brief pilgrimage, as a sign of the deep desire for true conversion, to the Holy Doors that are open in every Cathedral or in churches designated by the bishop in each diocese.

2. For those who are sick, elderly or alone where it is not possible for them to enter the Holy Door, the Jubilee Indulgence can be obtained by "living with faith and joyful hope this moment of trial, receiving Communion or attending Holy Mass and community prayer," as Pope Francis stated.

3. For those who are incarcerated, whose freedom is limited, they may obtain the Indulgence in the chapels of the prisons. Francis also said, "May the gesture of directing their thought and prayer to the Father each time they cross the threshold of their

* From the official document of the Vatican in announcing the Jubilee Year of Mercy. Quotes are from Pope Francis.

cell signify for them their passage through the Holy Door, because the mercy of God is able to transform hearts, and is also able to transform bars into an experience of freedom."

4. The Jubilee Indulgence may also be obtained by the faithful by performing one or more of the following corporal or spiritual works of mercy:

The corporal works of mercy are:

- **To feed the hungry;**
- **To give drink to the thirsty;**
- **To clothe the naked;**
- **To shelter the homeless;**
- **To visit the sick;**
- **To visit the imprisoned;**
- **To bury the dead.**

The spiritual works of mercy are:

- **To instruct the ignorant;**
- **To counsel the doubtful;**
- **To admonish sinners;**
- **To bear wrongs patiently;**
- **To forgive offenses willingly;**
- **To comfort the afflicted;**
- **To pray for the living and the dead.**

5. The Jubilee Indulgence can also be obtained for the deceased. When we remember them in the Eucharistic celebration, we pray for them "that the merciful Face of the Father free them of every remnant of fault and strongly embrace them in the unending beatitude."

6. For those who have had an abortion, the Holy Father "concedes to all priests for the Jubilee Year the discretion to absolve of the sin of abortion those who have procured it and who, with contrite heart, seek forgiveness for it. May priests fulfill this great task by expressing words of genuine welcome combined with a reflection that explains the gravity of the sin committed, besides indicating a path of authentic conversion by which to obtain the true and generous forgiveness of the Father."

7. The Jubilee Indulgence can also be obtained for all those who help to spread the Year of Mercy and in encouraging others on how to live the Year of Mercy. (Spreading this small book is an easy way to obtain this grace.)

CHAPTER FOUR

A Special Invitation by A Friend of Medjugorje & the Community of Caritas To Help You Live the Year of Mercy

1. **Join the Caritas Community in a 54-Day Rosary Novena—to prepare for the Jubilee Indulgence.** In order to live this special Year of Mercy in prayer and penance, A Friend of Medjugorje and the Community of Caritas wish to invite our friends and supporters across the world to join us in praying a special 54-Day Rosary Novena in preparation for going through the Holy Doors to obtain the Jubilee indulgence. This is open to everyone, even if you have already gone through the Holy Doors this year. Remember, you can get the Plenary Indulgence several times during the year, even on a regular basis, for souls in purgatory besides yourself. Experience has taught us that the more we put into preparing to receive a grace, the more powerful the grace is that we receive. Our Lady

has said, even when an intention is granted the more prayer attached to it, the greater the grace will be.

August 18, 1982

> **"...The more you believe firmly, the more you pray and fast for the same intention, the greater is the grace and the mercy of God..."**

The Caritas Community began the novena on Tuesday, March 22 and will <u>end</u> it on Saturday, the **Vigil of Pentecost**, May 14. **You can begin the novena at anytime during the year but you must start no later than September 27 in order to complete the 54-Day Rosary Novena before the Holy Doors close on November 20, 2016.** To end the novena, the Community will go through the Holy Doors of our diocese, but everyone participating in the novena will choose the Holy Doors closest to their homes. Special intentions will be offered during the novena that you can read on pages 63–64. We were given a beautiful affirmation of the importance of initiating this 54-Day Rosary Novena in this Year of Mercy when, just as this publication was ready to go to press, on <u>Saturday</u> morning, February 20, the Community randomly picked the following message at Morning Prayer. The <u>Words from Heaven</u> book stated:

June 2, 1984

Today is '<u>Saturday</u>', one of the days during which *the Novena to the Holy Spirit* (**prior to Pentecost**) is being conducted. The message to Marija is:

> **"Dear children, tonight I wish to tell you during the days of this novena to pray for the outpouring of the Holy Spirit on your families and on your parish. Pray, and you shall not regret it. God will give you gifts by which you will glorify Him till the end of your life on this earth. Thank you for having responded to my call."**

This should be a big encouragement for everyone to put their heart in this novena for what Our Lady desires to give in return. Though we would like as many people as possible to pray the novena with us that we can all benefit from the power of united prayer, if anyone receives this small book after the novena has started, you are still encouraged to pray the novena on your own.

SPECIAL ANNOUNCEMENT!

A Special Grace: Opening of the Bedroom of Apparitions

Make a Pilgrimage to Caritas and go through the "holy doors" of the Bedroom of Apparitions. Along with the 54 day Rosary novena, the Community of Caritas is inviting friends and followers of the Queen of Peace of Medjugorje to make a pilgrimage to the Bedroom and Field of Apparitions during this Holy Year! A Friend of Medjugorje and his wife are graciously allowing their home to be opened for the first time on designated dates, once each month, starting in April through November for the year 2016 so that pilgrims may come and pray in the Bedroom of Apparitions! For the Community of Caritas, the double doors that open into the Bedroom are "holy doors" as well, not by way of the Church designating them as holy, as at shrines and in basilicas and cathedrals, but by way of knowing we have entered into a room, through these doors, where the Queen of

Heaven has visited this room 144 times over the past 28 years. It is Her presence that has made them holy. There is powerful grace present within the walls of this special room that Our Lady, Herself, chose to manifest a special plan of God. Thousands* have been intimately touched, not only in the heart, but within their very soul while praying in the Bedroom. **During this Year of Mercy, when the Bedroom is opened, pilgrims will have the opportunity to consecrate or re-consecrate themselves to Our Lady when they will be present in the Bedroom.**

The Bedroom of Apparitions will be opened on the first or second Saturday of the following months, with the exception of the month of April, which will be opened on the first Friday

12:00 P.M. (after Rosary in the Field) to 6:00 P.M. (CST)

Saturday, May 7, 2016	**Saturday, September 3, 2016**
Saturday, June 4, 2016	**Saturday, October 8, 2016**
Saturday, July 9, 2016	**Saturday, November 5, 2016**
Saturday, August 6, 2016	

---

* Well over 100,000 people have prayed in the Bedroom of Apparitions through Marija's stays at the home, which the number of apparitions has amounted to nearly 2/3 of a year altogether. A lot of history has happened in regards to the last apparitions on earth.

While making a pilgrimage to Caritas, St. Paul's Cathedral in Birmingham is the location of the Holy Doors in the Birmingham diocese and we would strongly encourage everyone to make that a part of their pilgrimage in order to obtain the Jubilee Indulgence.*

2. **Spread the Year of Mercy through special materials provided by Caritas that will help to "stimulate interest" in the graces of the Holy Year as "bees feast upon flowers."** To make it as easy as possible to spread the information about the Year of Mercy, we have produced this small book containing all the essential information. It can be ordered in bulk and we encourage you to spread them to everyone you know. As previously stated, Pope Francis recently added yet another way to gain the Jubilee Indulgence. It can be gained by anyone who helps to spread knowledge about the Year of Mercy under the same conditions and requirements of the Holy Doors. Just by handing out these short books, you can gain an indulgence!

---

* Refer to page 54–56 to read the instructions for gaining the Indulgence.

CHAPTER FIVE

Intentions for the 54-Day Rosary Novena for the Year of Mercy

Pray these five intentions __Daily__ during the 54-Day Rosary Novena:

1. Dear Mother, with this novena, we pray for the grace to enter into deep prayer and reflection to prepare to make a holy Confession and obtain true sorrow for the sins we have committed and deep gratitude for the grace being received in this Year of Mercy. Before going through the Holy Doors, we pray for a complete detachment from sin, even venial sins, so that we may have a full remittance of the penalty of the sins of our past.

2. We come also, dear Mother, to plead the mercy of God upon our nation. We pray this Year of Mercy will lead to a GREAT outpouring of the Holy Spirit upon our nation — in every individual, family, community, and church. We pray this grace especially for our own loved ones, for those who have left the Church, and those who are far from the Heart of God.

3. In this Year of Mercy, we give to you, our Queen, the presidential election in the United States and beg your intercession in choosing the man best capable of seeing

the plans of God fulfilled in our nation. We know you said that peace will not come through the presidents, but we also recognize the significance of these next years of your apparitions and who is at the helm of this nation, as president, will have great bearing on all events that will unfold through Medjugorje and here. Bring to conversion this next president, that his reign will benefit Your plans. We pray for protection over him and ask that You would lead and guide his heart, to prepare him for the grave responsibilities he will inherit, and the heavy cross that will be placed upon his shoulders. As You did with George Washington* and Ronald Reagan,** give him supernatural signs of Your Motherly presence, that he will be filled with the confidence of God in leading this nation out of the shadows of death and into an era of peace, a peace that will spread from this nation to the rest of the world.

4. Lastly, our Queen, we pray for the grace to be ready, when the time of trial descends, that we may fulfill all that you desire of us as Your apostles in leading hearts to You, who will lead them to the Salvation of Your Son.

5. Personal intentions...

---

* See "American History You Never Learned" pgs. 19–27. To get a free copy visit the Caritas Mission House in Medjugorje, Bosnia-Hercegovina (see inside back cover for directions). Or visit **mej.com** and click on "Downloads."

** See <u>Look What Happened While You Were Sleeping</u>™ to learn how Our Lady revealed Herself to Pope Saint John Paul II and Ronald Reagan to bring down Communism, pgs. 444–463 in chapter 17. To get a free copy visit the Caritas Mission House in Medjugorje, Bosnia-Hercegovina (see inside back cover for directions). Or visit **mej.com** and click on "Downloads."

My Intentions:

_____

_____

_____

_____

_____

_____

_____

_____

_____

_____

_____

_____

_____

_____

_____

_____

_____

_____

My Intentions:

CHAPTER SIX

As an encouragement to have greater confidence in this Year of Mercy, we have included here the various promises Jesus made concerning devotion to the Divine Mercy revealed through St. Faustina.

Promises of Jesus Given To Those Who Trust in His Mercy

Through St. Faustina

Chaplet of Divine Mercy

See page 73

"Oh, what great graces I will grant to souls who say this chaplet; the very depths of My tender mercy are stirred for the sake of those who say the chaplet."

"At the hour of their death, I defend as My own glory every soul that will say this chaplet."

"…by saying the chaplet you are bringing mankind closer to Me."

"The souls that say this chaplet will be **embraced by My mercy during their lifetime and especially at the hour of their death."**

"When hardened sinners say [the chaplet], **I will fill their souls with peace, and the hour of their death will be a happy one.**"

"Through the chaplet **you will obtain everything**, if what you ask for is compatible with My will."

"Write that when they say this chaplet in the presence of the dying, **I will stand between My Father and the dying person, not as the just Judge but as the merciful Savior.**"

Prayer of Divine Mercy

See page 73

"Call upon My mercy on behalf of sinners; I desire their salvation. When you say this prayer, with a contrite heart and with faith on behalf of some sinner, **I will give him the grace of conversion.** This is the prayer: **O Blood and Water, which gushed forth from the Heart of Jesus as a fount of mercy for us, I trust in You.**"

Hour of Mercy

"I remind you, My daughter, that as often as you hear the clock strike the third hour, immerse yourself completely in My mercy, adoring and glorifying it; invoke its omnipotence for the whole world, and particularly for poor sinners; for at that moment mercy was opened wide for every soul. **In this hour you can obtain everything for yourself and for others for the asking**; it was the hour of grace for the whole world—mercy triumphed over justice."

"At three o'clock, implore My mercy, especially for sinners; and, if only for a brief moment, immerse yourself in My Passion, particularly in My abandonment at the moment of agony. This is the hour of great mercy for the whole world. I will allow you to enter into My mortal sorrow. **In this hour, I will refuse nothing to the soul that makes a request of Me.**"

<u>Image of Divine Mercy</u>

See page 72

"By means of this image **I shall grant many graces to souls.** It is to be a reminder of the demands of My mercy, because even the strongest faith is of no avail without works."

"Not in the beauty of the color, nor of the brush lies the greatness of this image, **but in My grace.**"

"I am offering people **a vessel with which they are to keep coming for graces to the fountain of mercy.** That vessel is this image with the signature: **'Jesus, I trust in You.'**"

"By means of this Image **I shall be granting many graces to souls**; so let every soul have access to it."

"Let the rays of grace enter your soul; **they bring with them light, warmth, and life.**"

Feast of Divine Mercy

The Feast of Divine mercy is always the Sunday after Easter

"I desire that the Feast of Mercy be a refuge and shelter for all souls, and especially for poor sinners. On that day the very depths of My tender mercy are open. I pour out a whole ocean of graces upon those souls who approach the fount of My mercy. The soul that will go to Confession and receive Holy Communion **shall obtain complete forgiveness of sins and punishment.** On that day all the divine floodgates through which graces flow are opened…The Feast of My Mercy has issued forth from My very depths for the consolation of the whole world."

Novena of Divine Mercy

See page 74

"By this novena, **I will grant every possible grace to souls.**"

"I will deny nothing to any soul whom you will bring to the fount of My mercy."

Those Who Spread Devotion of Divine Mercy

"All those souls who will glorify My mercy and spread its worship, encouraging others to trust in My mercy, **will not experience terror at the hour of death. My mercy will shield them in that final battle.**"

"Souls who spread the honor of My mercy **I shield through their entire lives as a tender mother her infant, and at the hour of death I will not be a Judge for them, but the Merciful Savior.** At that last hour, a soul has nothing with which to defend itself except My mercy. Happy is the soul that during its lifetime immersed itself in the Fountain of Mercy, because justice will have no hold on it."

"Who will proclaim My great mercy... **I shall protect them Myself at the hour of death, as My own glory.**"

"For your sake **I will withhold the hand which punishes**; for your sake **I bless the earth.**"

Promise of Mercy

"I perform works of mercy in every soul. The greater the sinner, the greater the right he has to My mercy. My mercy is confirmed in every work of My hands. He who trusts in My mercy will not perish, for all his affairs are Mine, and his enemies will be shattered at the base of My footstool."

"If a soul does not exercise mercy somehow or other, it will not obtain My mercy on the day of judgement. Oh, if only souls knew how to gather eternal treasure for themselves, they would not be judged, for **they would forestall My judgement with their mercy."**

Jesus, I Trust in You

CHAPTER SEVEN

Prayers for Divine Mercy

The Chaplet of Divine Mercy

The chaplet of Divine Mercy can be prayed at anytime but it is the most efficacious to pray it at 3:00 p.m. during the hour of mercy.

Say this prayer on ordinary Rosary beads:

First say one:

Our Father, Hail Mary, Apostle's Creed.

Then on the large beads of a Rosary, say the following words:

" Eternal Father, I offer You the Body and Blood, Soul and Divinity of Your dearly beloved Son, Our Lord Jesus Christ, in atonement for our sins and those of the whole world."

On the smaller beads, say the following words:

" For the sake of His sorrowful passion have mercy on us and on the whole world."

In conclusion, say these words three times:

" Holy God, Holy Mighty One, Holy Immortal One, have mercy on us and on the whole world."

Prayer of Divine Mercy

Closing Prayer, say three times:

" O Blood and Water, which gushed forth from the Heart of Jesus as a fount of Mercy for us, I trust in You!

Divine Mercy Novena

The Novena, as requested by Our Lord, begins on Good Friday, and ends on the vigil of the Feast of Divine Mercy each year. However, you can pray the novena throughout the year as well.

It is greatly recommended that the following novena intentions and prayer be said together with the Chaplet of Divine Mercy, since Our Lord specifically asked for a novena of Chaplets, especially before the Feast of Mercy.

First Day

Today bring to Me

ALL MANKIND, ESPECIALLY ALL SINNERS,

and immerse them in the ocean of My mercy. In this way you will console Me in the bitter grief into which the loss of souls plunges Me.

Most Merciful Jesus, whose very nature it is to have compassion on us and to forgive us, do not look upon our sins but upon our trust which we place in Your infinite goodness. Receive us all into the abode of Your Most Compassionate Heart, and never let us escape from It. We beg this of You by Your love which unites You to the Father and the Holy Spirit.

Eternal Father, turn Your merciful gaze upon all mankind and especially upon poor sinners, all enfolded in the Most Compassionate Heart of Jesus, For the sake of His sorrowful Passion show us Your mercy, that we may praise the omnipotence of Your mercy forever and ever. Amen.

Second Day

Today bring to Me

THE SOULS OF PRIESTS AND RELIGIOUS,

and immerse them in My unfathomable mercy. It was they who gave Me strength to endure My bitter Passion. Through them as through channels My mercy flows out upon mankind.

Most Merciful Jesus, from whom comes all that is good, increase Your grace in men and women consecrated to Your service, that they may perform worthy works of mercy; and that all who see them may glorify the Father of Mercy who is in Heaven.

Eternal Father, turn Your merciful gaze upon the company of chosen ones in Your vineyard—upon the souls of priests and religious; and endow them with the strength of Your blessing. For the love of the Heart of Your Son in which they are enfolded, impart to them Your power and light, that they may be able to guide others in the way of salvation and with one voice sing praise to Your boundless mercy for ages without end. Amen.

Third Day

Today bring to Me

ALL DEVOUT AND FAITHFUL SOULS,

and immerse them in the ocean of My mercy. These souls brought Me consolation on the Way of the Cross. They were that drop of consolation in the midst of an ocean of bitterness.

Most Merciful Jesus, from the treasury of Your mercy, You impart Your graces in great abundance to each and all. Receive us into the abode of Your Most Compassionate Heart and never let us escape from It. We beg this grace of You by that Most wondrous love for the heavenly Father with which Your Heart burns so fiercely.

Eternal Father, turn Your merciful gaze upon faithful souls, as upon the inheritance of Your Son. For the sake of His sorrowful Passion, grant them Your blessing and surround them with Your constant protection. Thus may they never fail in love or lose the treasure of the holy faith, but rather, with all the hosts of Angels and Saints, may they glorify Your boundless mercy for endless ages. Amen.

Fourth Day

Today bring to Me

THOSE WHO DO NOT BELIEVE IN GOD* AND
THOSE WHO DO NOT YET KNOW ME.,

**and immerse them in My unfathomable mercy. It was
they who gave Me strength to endure My bitter Passion.
Through them as through channels My mercy flows out
upon mankind.**

Most compassionate Jesus, you are the Light of the
whole world. Receive into the abode of Your Most Compassionate Heart the souls of those who do not believe in God
and of those who as yet do not know You. Let the rays of Your
grace enlighten them that they, too, together with us, may
extol Your wonderful mercy; and do not let them escape from
the abode which is Your Most Compassionate Heart.

Eternal Father, turn Your merciful gaze upon the souls
of those who do not believe in You, and of those who as yet
do not know You, but who are enclosed in the Most Compassionate Heart of Jesus. Draw them to the light of the Gospel.
These souls do not know what great happiness it is to love You.
Grant that they, too, may extol the generosity of Your mercy
for endless ages. Amen.

---

* Our Lord's original words here were "the pagans." Since the pontificate of Pope
John XXIII, the Church has seen fit to replace this term with clearer and more
appropriate terminology.

Fifth Day

Today bring to Me

THE SOULS OF THOSE WHO HAVE SEPARATED THEMSELVES FROM MY CHURCH,*

and immerse them in the ocean of My mercy. During My bitter Passion they tore at My Body and Heart, that is, My Church. As they return to unity with the Church My wounds heal and in this way they alleviate My Passion.

Most Merciful Jesus, Goodness Itself, You do not refuse light to those who seek it of You. Receive into the abode of your Most Compassionate Heart the souls of those who have separated themselves from Your Church. Draw them by Your light into the unity of the Church, and do not let them escape from the abode of Your Most Compassionate Heart; but bring it about that they, too, come to glorify the generosity of Your mercy.

Eternal Father, turn Your merciful gaze upon the souls of those who have separated themselves from your Son's Church, who have squandered Your blessings and misused

---

* Our Lord's original words here were "heretics and schismatics," since He spoke to St. Faustina within the context of her times. As of the Second Vatican Council, Church authorities have seen fit not to use those designations in accordance with the explanation given in the Council's Decree on Ecumenism. Every pope since the Council has reaffirmed that usage. St. Faustina herself, her heart always in harmony with the mind of the Church, most certainly would have agreed. When at one time, because of the decisions of her superiors and father confessor, she was not able to execute Our Lady's inspirations and orders, she declared: "I will follow Your will insofar as You will permit me to do so through your representative. O my Jesus, I give priority to the voice of the Church over the voice with which You speak to me."(487). The Lord confirmed her action and praised her for it.

Your graces by obstinately persisting in their errors. Do not look upon their errors, but upon the love of Your own Son and upon His bitter Passion, which He underwent for their sake, since they, too, are enclosed in His Most Compassionate Heart. Bring it about that they also may glorify your great mercy for endless ages. Amen.

Sixth Day

Today bring to Me

THE MEEK AND HUMBLE SOULS AND THE SOULS OF LITTLE CHILDREN,

and immerse them in My mercy. These souls most closely resemble My Heart. They strengthened Me during My bitter agony. I saw them as earthly Angels, who will keep vigil at My altars. I pour out upon them whole torrents of grace. Only the humble soul is capable of receiving My grace. I favor humble souls with My confidence.

Most Merciful Jesus, You yourself have said, "Learn from Me for I am meek and humble of heart." Receive into the abode of Your Most Compassionate Heart all meek and humble souls and the souls of little children. These souls send all heaven into ecstasy and they are the heavenly Father's favorites. They are a sweet-smelling bouquet before the throne of God; God himself takes delight in their fragrance. These souls have a permanent abode in your Most Compassionate Heart, O Jesus, and they unceasingly sing out a hymn of love and mercy.

Eternal Father, turn Your merciful gaze upon meek souls, upon humble souls, and upon little children who are enfolded in the abode which is the Most Compassionate Heart of Jesus. These souls bear the closest resemblance to Your Son. Their fragrance rises from the earth and reaches Your very throne. Father of mercy and of all goodness, I beg You by the love You bear these souls and by the delight You take in them: Bless the whole world, that all souls together may sing out the praises of Your mercy for endless ages. Amen.

Seventh Day

Today bring to Me

THE SOULS WHO ESPECIALLY VENERATE AND GLORIFY MY MERCY,*

and immerse them in My mercy. These souls sorrowed most over My Passion and entered most deeply into My spirit. They are living images of My Compassionate Heart.

---

* The text leads one to conclude that in the first prayer directed to Jesus, who is the Redeemer, it is "victim" souls and contemplatives that are being prayed for; those persons, that is, that voluntarily offered themselves to God for the salvation of their neighbor. This explains their close union with the Savior and the extraordinary efficacy that their invisible activity has for others. In the second prayer, directed to the Father from whom comes "every worthwhile gift and every genuine benefit," we recommend the "active" souls, who promote devotion to The Divine Mercy and exercise with it all the other works that lend themselves to the spiritual and material uplifting of their brethren.

These souls will shine with a special brightness in the next life. Not one of them will go into the fire of hell. I shall particularly defend each one of them at the hour of death.

Most Merciful Jesus, whose Heart is Love Itself, receive into the abode of Your Most Compassionate Heart the souls of those who particularly extol and venerate the greatness of Your mercy. These souls are mighty with the very power of God Himself. In the midst of all afflictions and adversities they go forward, confident of Your mercy; and united to You, O Jesus, they carry all mankind on their shoulders. These souls will not be judged severely, but Your mercy will embrace them as they depart from this life.

Eternal Father, turn Your merciful gaze upon the souls who glorify and venerate Your greatest attribute, that of Your fathomless mercy, and who are enclosed in the Most Compassionate Heart of Jesus. These souls are a living Gospel; their hands are full of deeds of mercy, and their hearts, overflowing with joy, sing a canticle of mercy to You, O Most High! I beg You O God: Show them Your mercy according to the hope and trust they have placed in You. Let there be accomplished in them the promise of Jesus, who said to them that during their life, but especially at the hour of death, the souls who will venerate this fathomless mercy of His, He, Himself, will defend as His glory. Amen.

Eighth Day

Today bring to Me

THE SOULS WHO ARE DETAINED IN PURGATORY,

and immerse them in the abyss of My mercy. Let the torrents of My Blood cool down their scorching flames. All these souls are greatly loved by Me. They are making retribution to My justice. It is in your power to bring them relief. Draw all the indulgences from the treasury of My Church and offer them on their behalf. Oh, if you only knew the torments they suffer, you would continually offer for them the alms of the spirit and pay off their debt to My justice.

Most Merciful Jesus, You Yourself have said that You desire mercy; so I bring into the abode of Your Most Compassionate Heart the souls in Purgatory, souls who are very dear to You, and yet, who must make retribution to Your justice. May the streams of Blood and Water which gushed forth from your Heart put out the flames of Purgatory, that there, too, the power of Your mercy may be celebrated.

Eternal Father, turn Your merciful gaze upon the souls suffering in Purgatory, who are enfolded in the Most Compassionate Heart of Jesus. I beg You, by the sorrowful Passion of Jesus Your Son, and by all the bitterness with which His most sacred Soul was flooded: Manifest Your mercy to the souls who are under Your just scrutiny. Look upon them in no other way but only through the Wounds of Jesus, Your dearly beloved Son; for we firmly believe that there is no limit to Your goodness and compassion. Amen.

Ninth Day

Today bring to Me
SOULS WHO HAVE BECOME LUKEWARM,*

and immerse them in the abyss of My mercy. These souls wound My Heart most painfully. My soul suffered the most dreadful loathing in the Garden of Olives because of lukewarm souls. They were the reason I cried out: "Father, take this cup away from Me, if it be Your will." For them the last hope of salvation is to run to My mercy.

Most compassionate Jesus, You are Compassion Itself. I bring lukewarm souls into the abode of Your Most Compassionate Heart. In this fire of Your pure love let these tepid souls, who, like corpses, filled You with such deep loathing, be once again set aflame. O Most Compassionate Jesus, exercise the omnipotence of Your mercy and draw them into the very ardor of Your love, and bestow upon them the gift of holy love, for nothing is beyond Your power.

---

* To understand who are the souls designated for this day, and who in the Diary are called "lukewarm," but are also compared to ice and to corpses, we would do well to take note of the definition that the Savior Himself gave them when speaking to St. Faustina about them on one occasion: **There are souls who thwart My efforts** (1682). **Souls without love or devotion, souls full of egoism and selfishness, proud and arrogant souls who have just enough warmth to keep themselves alive: My Heart cannot bear this. All the graces that I pour out upon them flow off them as off the face of a rock. I cannot stand them because they are neither good nor bad** (1702).

Eternal Father, turn Your merciful gaze upon lukewarm souls who are nonetheless enfolded in the Most Compassionate Heart of Jesus. Father of Mercy, I beg You by the bitter Passion of Your Son and by His three-hour agony on the Cross: Let them, too, glorify the abyss of Your mercy. Amen.

CHAPTER EIGHT

A Plea to Our Lady

In an interview with A Friend in Medjugorje in March, 1996, Medjugorje visionary Mirjana revealed that she had received a special prayer from Our Lady and had been praying it since 1987. Our Lady told Mirjana that this prayer is connected to the secrets and that one day Mirjana will be told by Our Lady to release the prayer to everyone. That time has not yet come. The prayer is a prayer for nonbelievers, or as Our Lady says, those who have not experienced the love of God. It is a prayer that once it is released, will spread like wildfire around the world and will lead a massive amount of souls to conversion.

After this meeting with Mirjana, A Friend of Medjugorje wrote, *"Medjugorje, Mirjana, A Mystery Is Revealed,"* in which he reflected upon what Our Lady wants to accomplish through this new prayer that is connected to the secrets. Studying the supernatural grace attached to other sacramentals that Our Lady initiated in other apparitions, namely the Rosary, the Miraculous Medal and the Brown Scapular—and the miracles that abounded through the use of these powerfully anointed sacramentals, he grasped the power of what awaits the world with the coming release of this new sacramental that Our Lady taught Mirjana to pray.

A Friend of Medjugorje wrote a prayer entitled, **Prayer for Nonbelievers,** in which he entreats Our Lady to not wait long, but to release the secret prayer that *"the dam of love, of God's mercy, will break forth"* and *"as the rivers fill the oceans, Your love of God will fill the earth."* In the prayers we offer in this Extraordinary Year of Mercy, we wanted to include the **Prayer for Nonbelievers** in the hope that we can win for the world this extraordinary grace, perhaps even earlier than what God has intended. This is the year to demand boldly for graces from Heaven. We invite you to join us in praying it in your daily prayers and when you attend Mass. With our voices raised in heartfelt prayer for this intention, together let us bring about this miracle prayer for the world.

August 2, 2011

> **"… I call you to gather into God's family and to be strengthened with the Father's strength. As individuals, my children, you cannot stop the evil that wants to begin to rule in this world and to destroy it. But, according to God's will, <u>all together</u>, with my Son, you can change everything and <u>heal the world</u>…"**

Prayer for Nonbelievers

Come Mary,
Come tomorrow again and again.
We will pray with you.

Bring back our loved ones
Who have left the Church,
Those who have left God.

We will join you on the second of each month.
We will pray for greater graces
To be attached to your intention.

We will pray that the dam of love,
Of God's mercy, will break forth,
That your new prayer be released soon.

We will pray that it will flow out
As a river to all the nations,
That as the rivers fill the oceans,
Your love of God will fill the earth.

We wait.
We anticipate that great day,
And we call you as you have called us,
To add our prayers, fasting, and sacrifices
To Mirjana's in order that you may
Obtain all your wishes for the world.

O loving Mother,
Thank you for the gift
That the world is on the brink of receiving!

A Friend of Medjugorje

A Special Grace: Opening of the Bedroom of Apparitions

Make a Pilgrimage to Caritas and go through the "holy doors" of the Bedroom of Apparitions.

Directions to Caritas & the Cathedral of St. Paul

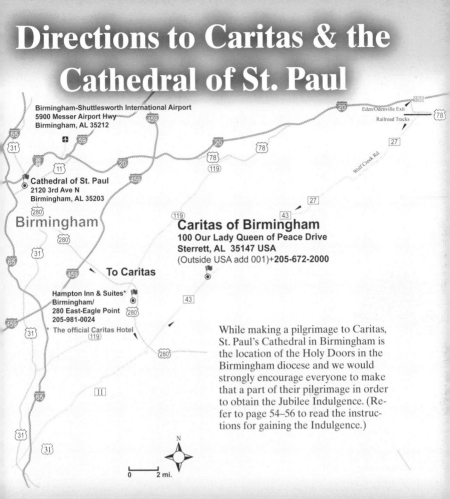

Birmingham-Shuttlesworth International Airport
5900 Messer Airport Hwy
Birmingham, AL 35212

Cathedral of St. Paul
2120 3rd Ave N
Birmingham, AL 35203

Birmingham

Caritas of Birmingham
100 Our Lady Queen of Peace Drive
Sterrett, AL 35147 USA
(Outside USA add 001)+**205-672-2000**

To Caritas

Hampton Inn & Suites*
Birmingham/
280 East-Eagle Point
205-981-0024
The official Caritas Hotel

Eden/Odenville Exit
Railroad Tracks
Wolf Creek Rd.

While making a pilgrimage to Caritas, St. Paul's Cathedral in Birmingham is the location of the Holy Doors in the Birmingham diocese and we would strongly encourage everyone to make that a part of their pilgrimage in order to obtain the Jubilee Indulgence. (Refer to page 54–56 to read the instructions for gaining the Indulgence.)

N

0   2 mi.

The Bedroom of Apparitions will be opened on the first or second Saturday of the following months, with the exception of the month of April, which will be opened on the first Friday

12:00 P.M. (after Rosary in the Field) to 6:00 P.M. (CST)

Saturday, May 7, 2016
Saturday, June 4, 2016
Saturday, July 9, 2016
Saturday, August 6, 2016

Saturday, September 3, 2016
Saturday, October 8, 2016
Saturday, November 5, 2016

BVM Caritas Medjugorje Pilgrimages

Think about it.

If you could combine every single event for the past 34 years that occurred in Washington D.C., New York, Los Angeles, Chicago, Paris, London and every other place in the world, it would be dwarfed by the event of one single day in Medjugorje. Our Lady, Mary, Mother of Christ, comes to the earth, blesses the whole world with Her presence and speaks to us with words conveyed directly from God. Wouldn't you like to be part of one of the most important events in the history of creation?

Why pilgrimage with BVM Caritas Medjugorje Pilgrimages?

* The experience of over 542 trips to Medjugorje!

* Combined experience of over 675 years!

* By the testimonies of our pilgrims, it is repeatedly stated that Caritas is the most spiritual!

* Lowest Fares of anybody for a full-hosted pilgrimage!

* Non-smoking trips (many who smoke and travel with us, offer it up as a sacrifice and receive many graces).

* The Community of Caritas lives in Medjugorje which gives us an in-depth, behind-the-scenes understanding of Medjugorje.

* Sites are prayed at, shown and explained (such as the site where Jakov and Vicka were physically and bodily taken to Heaven from Earth by Our Lady).

* The only interest we have is spiritual profit. None of us are paid to guide you. We do it in response to Our Lady's message in which She requested to **"…sacrifice your lives for the salvation of the world…"** (February 25, 1988)

"This was my second experience with Caritas in Medjugorje and if I have the means, it won't be my last."

D.R., Baton Rouge, Louisiana, April 2015 Pilgrim

✳ Our mission house in Medjugorje distributes our materials to all who come from around the world. You will benefit on your pilgrimage by the spiritual material, advice, and guidance that will be available to you.

✳ You stay in the middle of the village by St. James Church, yet on the trail to Apparition Hill ✧**a best location!**✧ On top of that, pilgrimages are scheduled around special apparitions or being in the village when the monthly message to the world is given.

✳ BVM CARITAS MEDJUGORJE PILGRIMAGES has remained loyal and centered exclusively on Medjugorje, and pilgrimages only to this holy village. Focus and prayer life has given our founder a deep understanding about Our Lady's apparitions and formed this understanding in all who lead the pilgrimages from the community.

This year, why not visit the village that is changing the entire world?

Please call
BVM CARITAS MEDJUGORJE PILGRIMAGES
for more details on your full package:
205-672-2000, ext. 218 24hr.

Check out
mej.com
click pilgrimages on the left menu
The most extensive Medjugorje website in the world.
Sign up for the mejList free to be kept updated

We Must Go to
A Higher Truth

By A Friend of Medjugorje

Thirty-Four Years of Apparitions
1981-2015 A.D.

"What a clear and strong writing! A Friend of Medjugorje has clarified questions from the past, present and future regarding the apparitions of Our Lady of Medjugorje. Thank you."

Kathy
Marion, Ohio USA

With 34 years of growth in understanding Medjugorje, we can now say we understand Medjugorje to a greater degree. We can say, "Our Lady is here in a new way that has never been seen in the history of the Church and She is bringing us to a higher Truth." What does that statement mean? Why is this necessary? Why do others stand in my way? Why do they say *"Go to the back of the bus. You are not allowed here up in the front."* What are we to say, what are we to do?

These questions and more are answered in this short read giving you simple straightforward answers. "We Must go to A Higher Truth"

Call Caritas 205-672-2000 or go to **Medjugorje.com** and click on MejMart

Medjugorje.com

The #1 Most Popular Medjugorje Website in the World.

- The most looked to site for direction on the messages given by Our Lady of Medjugorje

- Latest updates on Medjugorje

- Most extensive history of the apparitions: Beginning days, the 10 secrets, signs and miracles, etc.

- *RadioWAVE*™: Hosted by A Friend of Medjugorje, listened to by people all over the world.

- *mejList*: the Free Medjugorje newsletter

- Send your petition to Medjugorje and have it presented to Our Lady during the apparition

- Free downloads: audio, books and booklets

Dear Caritas,

"Thank you and many of God's blessings on a
purely soul-saving site!"

R.C.

Dear Caritas,

"I just wanted you to know how thankful we are for all you do
with Medjugorje.com. We found your site almost 1 year ago.
My wife and I have followed Our Lady's Messages ever since.
My life has changed. We just want to personally thank you for
loving Our Lady so very much."

T. & K. C.

Conversion is not a one-time experience. It is a process of daily growing closer and closer to God. This writing is for all those who have known the joy and sweetness of the call of God, as well as the struggles, heartache, sorrow, and frustration that come once the "honeymoon" is over and the time comes when one must "work" to maintain their relationship with God. How does one maintain conversion in the midst of the world, difficulties and their sufferings? Can one ever rediscover the sweetness of their beginning days of their call? Discover the answer to these questions, as well as others you may have in regard to what Our Lady is asking when She calls us to conversion.

TREASURE CHEST

By A Friend of Medjugorje

OUR LADY HAS SAID IF WE WANT TO understand the reason for Her coming as well as to know how God deals with His people, we should read Sacred Scripture everyday. She also has said to read the lives of the saints. What we learn by being obedient to Our Lady's advice is that God never abandons His people but always gives grace to help us return to the way of salvation.

BKIOIO

Within these pages you will discover the continuation of God's mercy for His people… but now it is "*we*" who are being written into that history. It is "*our*" lives that God's tender heart is directed towards. And it is Our Lady whom He has sent to be the Herald of His mercy to "*our*" world, not just for the present children, but for children in all future generations as well.

Within the event of Medjugorje there are still many mysteries left to be revealed. One of these mysteries deals directly with "*new*" prayers which Our Lady has taught to Mirjana and Vicka for the conversion of many souls. How privileged we are to be the "*witnesses*" of these extraordinary events in these extraordinary times.

MEDJUGORJE,

Mirjana,

A MYSTERY IS REVEALED

America was given a beautiful gift

on Thanksgiving Day, November 24, 1988.

The Virgin Mary appeared in an open field, consecrating the spot by Her Heavenly visitation. She announced, through the Medjugorje visionary Marija Lunetti, She was here to help us and that She would **"…intercede for you to God for all your intentions."** Experience Our Lady, experience retreat, experience Christmas, experience a place fragranced by the Queen of the Angels Herself and leave moved deep within your heart. With Our Lady appearing over thirty-three years in Medjugorje, come to a special place She's visited one hundred eighty-one times and allow Our Lady to enlighten you in regard to God's plans to renew the face of the earth…nay, even all of creation.

We invite you to an experience of a lifetime.

Come to the five-day, annual retreat of conversion that will not only recharge you but change your life.

Check out

mej.com

Follow the events of December 8–12 as they happen.

~Annually~

December 8th–12th

For more information, call:
205-672-2000 ext. 218

Or write:
Caritas of Birmingham
100 Our Lady Queen of Peace Drive
Sterrett, Alabama 35147-9987 USA

Five "Must Do's" in Medjugorje

Apparition Mountain, Cross Mountain, the Visionaries, St. James Church, and the Caritas Mission House, these are the five "**must do's**" to have a complete Medjugorje pilgrimage. Throughout the years, pilgrims from every nation have made the Caritas of Birmingham Mission House in Medjugorje a part of their pilgrimage. Countless numbers have relayed to us that it is there, in the Mission House, where they came to understand more fully Our Lady's messages and plans for the world. It is why people, who have returned home from their pilgrimages, have told others going to Medjugorje to go to the Caritas Mission House, stating that the Caritas Mission House was a high point of their pilgrimage and a "**must do**" to make a pilgrimage to Medjugorje a complete and more profound experience.

Don't Miss a Visit to the Caritas Mission House

"We come in several times during our pilgrimages to talk about the messages with the community. We are always welcome and encouraged to bring others in as well. We have gone to Medjugorje many times and the Mission House is always a place we must visit."

B & G
Ireland

"The billboard drew me and my family into the Caritas Mission House. I was suprised to find the message and CD's in my language."

Family of 7 from Spain

"I came in looking for materials to take back to my convent and I left with 2 bags of beautiful booklets and postcards containing Our Lady's messages."

Nun from England

Look for the **St. Michael statue** and **"This is My Time" Signs**.
Caritas of Birmingham Mission House is operated by the Community of Caritas.
The Mother house is located at: **100 Our Lady Queen of Peace Drive**
Sterrett, Alabama 35147 USA

 Extensive up-to-date information on Medjugorje as it happens.

Other Titles About Our Lady's Messages!

If you would like more copies of this short book for distribution at your church, prayer group, or for family or friends, etc…please contact your local bookstore, call Caritas of Birmingham–24 hours a day, or fill out the order form at the end of this booklet.

Other titles in this series by A Friend of Medjugorje:

Books by A Friend of Medjugorje:

BF101 <u>Words from Heaven</u>®
Our Lady's messages from Medjugorje

    1 copy - $15.00
    5 copies - $11.00 ea
    10+copies - $10.00 ea

BF103 <u>How to Change Your Husband</u>™
BF104 <u>I See Far</u>™
Prices for <u>How to Change Your Husband</u> & <u>I See Far</u>

1 copy - $6.00	50 copies - $1.80 ea
5 copies - $4.00 ea	100 copies - $1.70 ea
10 copies - $3.00 ea	1000 copies - $1.40 ea
25 copies - $1.90 ea	

BF105 <u>Look What Happened While You Were Sleeping</u>™ $14.95 ea

BF108 <u>It Ain't Gonna Happen</u>™

1 copy — $15.00	100 copies — $2.80 ea
10 copies — $7.00 ea	500 copies — $1.00 ea
50 copies — $3.30 ea	1000 copies — $.95 ea

BF110 <u>They Fired the First Shot 2012</u>™ SOFT COVER $15.00 ea
    Special Soft Cover Case Pricing $5.00/bk 16 Books
    $80.00 + $30.00 S&H = $110.00

CD110MP3 <u>They Fired the First Shot 2012</u>™ MP3 AUDIO BOOK $5.00 ea
    10 copies — $15.00 ($1.50 ea)
    20 copies — $25.00 ($1.25 ea)
    100 copies — $50.00 (50¢ ea)

BF114 <u>Medjugorje Prepare the World for My Final Coming</u>™

1 copy — $2.00	100 copies — 70¢ ea
10 copies — 90¢ ea	500 copies — 60¢ ea
50 copies — 80¢ ea	1000 copies — 50¢ ea

Title list cont. on next page

Short Books by A Friend of Medjugorje:

BK1001 Whose Opinion is Right?
BK1002 Twenty Years of Apparitions
BK1003 American History You Never Learned
BK1004 Changing History
BK1005 Patriotic Rosary™ (1=free,10=90¢ea 25=75¢ea 50=60¢ea 100=40¢ea)
BK1006 August 5th, What Are You Doing for Her Birthday?
BK1007 Medjugorje—The Fulfillment of all Marian Apparitions
BK1008 A New Ark?
BK1009 As Go God's People, So Goes the World
BK1010 Medjugorje, Mirjana, A Mystery Revealed
BK1011 A Time for Decision
BK1012 satan Wants to Destroy Medjugorje
BK1013 Fasting
BK1014 Modesty
BK1015 In Front of the Crucifix with Our Lady
BK1016 Treasure Chest
BK1017 Entering A New Time
BK1018 Understanding Our Lady's Messages
BK1019 A Blessing to Help Save the World

Suggested Donation		
1 Copy	Free (pay only $5.00 S&H)	
10 Copies	$4.00	(40¢ ea.)
25 Copies	$8.75	(35¢ ea.)
50 Copies	$15.00	(30¢ ea.)
100 Copies	$25.00	(25¢ ea.)
1000 Copies	$200.00	(20¢ ea.)

BK1020 Fallen Field Angel
BK1021 Don't Tell Me What to Do!
BK1022 Spanning 2000 Years of History
BK1023 When You Decide for Change
BK1024 Have You Become Complacent or Fallen Asleep?
BK1025 I Don't Like My Cross
BK1026 What Do We Do Now?
BK1027 Thy Will Be Done? And Hand to the Plow
BK1028 Our Lady's 7 Steps to…Set the Captives Free
BK1029 Who's Driving?
BK1030 "I Don't Have to Go to Medjugorje." Reasons Why One Must Go to Medjugorje
BK1031 The Seven Novenas in Preparation for the Five Days of Prayer for the Reconciling
  of Ourselves, Our Families, and Our Nation Back to God
BK1033 Calling on Heaven (Caritas' prayers)
BK1034 Pieta Prayer Book (1=$1.00, 10=90¢EA, 25=80¢EA, 50=70¢EA, 100=60¢EA, 1,000=50¢EA)
BK1119 Pieta Prayer Book Large Print (1=$1.00, 10=90¢EA, 25=80¢EA, 50=70¢EA, 100=60¢EA)
BK1035 A Village Sees the Light (10¢ea)
BK1036 Our Lady's Formula for Victory: "Pray, Pray, Pray"
BK1037 A Miracle from the Field for Our Nation
BK1038 Crisis-Discipline
BK1039 Quietism
BK1040 Wedding Booklet
BK1041 Why So Many Disasters?
BK1042 How the Early Church Learned…
BK1043 Be Strong! Do Not Relax!
BK1044 Some Remarkable things About Our Lady's Messages
BK1045 You Have Been Called
BK1046 Two Americas
BK1047 Some Remarkable things About Our Lady's Messages
BK1048 Ready"ing" for the Storm
BK1049 Judge with Right Judgement

Volume orders can be made up of different booklets.

More short books are being produced monthly at Caritas of Birmingham, call 205-672-2000 for new titles.

Name _____ **Date** _____ **e-mail** _____

Address _____

City _____ **State** _____ **Zip** _____ **Phone #** _____ **Birthday** _____

Method of Payment: ☐ Check/Money Order ☐ Cash ☐ Visa ☐ MasterCard ☐ Discover

Card#: ☐☐☐☐ ☐☐☐☐ ☐☐☐☐ ☐☐☐☐ **Exp. Date:** ☐☐ - ☐☐ 3-Digit Code on Back: ☐☐☐ **Signature** _____

Caritas ID# _____ (Using your ID# will save at least one week of processing on your order in addition to saving this mission thousands of dollars a year. Please use your ID# which can be found above your address with each mailing received from Caritas, or call 205-672-2000.)

Title	Qty.	Price Ea.	Total
	Subtotal		
	S&H		
	Grand Total		

Short Book Suggested Donation

1 Copy	Free (pay only S&H)
10 Copies	$4.00 (40¢ EA.)
25 Copies	$8.75 (35¢ EA.)
50 Copies	$15.00 (30¢ EA.)
100 Copies	$15.00 (30¢ EA.)
100 Copies	$25.00 (25¢ EA.)
1000 Copies	$200.00 (20¢ EA.)

Shipping & Handling

Order Sub-total	U.S. Mail (Standard)	UPS (Faster)
$0-$10.00	$5.00	$10.00
$10.01-$20.00	$7.50	$12.50
$20.01-$50.00	$10.00	$15.00
$50.01-$100.00	$15.00	$20.00
Over $100.00	15% of total	20% of total

For overnight delivery, call for pricing. ***International (Surface): Double above shipping cost.
Call for faster International delivery.

Send Order and Donation to:

Caritas of Birmingham
100 Our Lady Queen of Peace Drive
Sterrett, AL 35147 USA

or call **205-672-2000 ext. 315** twenty four hours a day!

104